How to Live in a World That Is Dying

Meditations and Prayers for the Earth

Mary Jane Miller

How to Live in a World That Is Dying
Text and Layout | Mary Jane Miller
Editor | Sy Brontide
Book Design | Mel Ahlborn for Illumiation Studio
 www.millericons.com

ISBN 979-8-9886283-5-4

 How To Live In A World that is Dying?

MOTHER EARTH
HELP US
TO FEEL
YOUR PRESENCE
IN OUR
BEING
AND YOUR
ABUNDANT LIFE
ENERGY
COURSING
THROUGH ALL
OF CREATION.

WE NEED
TO EXPERIENCE
YOUR
RESONANT LOVE
AND FEEL
THE RAPTURE
OF
BEING ALIVE.

Introduction

I TITLED THE BOOK, HOW TO LIVE IN A WORLD THAT IS DYING? because I think it is prudent for our species to ask the question. From one end of the Earth to the other and on every continent humans can agree our world is in crisis. Our societal norms and traditions are dying. Our eco systems are collapsing. Species are dying and becoming extinct. We must ask ourselves, "Does humanity have the will to refrain from being a hindrance to Earth's sustainability and healthy existence?" People all over the world are living in an era, time, and place that is in a global, economic and environmental crisis. It is childish to imagine God will come down and fix it. I do believe humanity has and will play an increasing part in the organic design of this glorious world and all she has to offer.

HOW DO WE LIVE IN A DYING WORLD? This series of prayers and meditations are the result of my extensive contemplation surrounding this question. I offer this book as a resource and tool to encourage us to make time for personal and collective reflection. If we consider all the beauty around the globe, we cannot help but marvel and, ultimately, cherish it. We can be good stewards of this evolving mystery, from the astronomical majestic to the tiny microcosm that have thrived throughout the ages.

HUMANITY HAS ALWAYS OFFERED UP PRAYERS FOR THOSE IN NEED; the sick, the broken, and the homeless. From generation to generation we have prayed for our brothers and sisters, wives and children, parents and neighbors, but have we prayed enough for the environment, our Mother Earth, and God's Creation? We need to ask the hard question: "What part have I played in contributing to the crisis we are in today? What sacrifices have been made and provided for my existence?" The answers and confessions must be honest without excuses. It is time to slow down and profoundly reflect on our human history and behavior. We cannot go forward without a clear understanding of where we are and how we arrived here.

POPE FRANCIS ENCOURAGED FOLLOWERS AROUND THE WORLD TO PRAY. He instructed believers to reflect and pray for Our Earthly Home. He proposed that prayer and meditation aid in better understanding humanity's place on the planet and in the world. He added, "The Blessed Mother's intercession on behalf of the planet can bring humanity to realize deeply the love God bestowed on Earth for our benefit.

THERE IS MUCH TO BE DONE AND EVEN MORE TO READJUST. Like many people, I feel overwhelmed by the ecological crisis that continues to mount around the globe. Feelings of helplessness or hopelessness are expected as we reflect on the enormity of what is corrupted, hurting, and already lost. What can anyone person do to bring about change? I believe that prayer is a prudent place to begin. A few minutes of reflection every day has the power to shift our understanding of our purpose on the planet.

OUR MINDS AND HEARTS ARE VOLUMINOUS ORGANS that receive the in-pouring of mystical understanding. I believe that through the time-tested methods of prayer, contemplation, and meditation we can clear our minds and deepen our connections to each other and the world we live in. My hope is that this book will be a guide that brings our wants and desires into alignment with the marvelous energy that has designed Creation.

Creating a Prayer Practice

HOW DO WE CREATE A CONSISTENT PRAYER PRACTICE? Virtually every major religious tradition uses some form of sacred ritual and ceremony to connect to an energy greater than themselves. Ritual, sacrament, and sacred spaces remind us to participate and focus our intent. The call to pray without ceasing is a call to all of humanity to remember and ethically comprehend our place on the planet.

CHRISTIANS, HINDUS, JEWS, BUDDHISTS, SUFI MYSTICS, and others have used mantras and prayers to aid their devotions. For centuries, people around the globe have used candles, music, a string of knots, prayer beads, tarot cards, or rune stones to anchor the mind. Most traditions encourage choosing specific places and times to aid their prayer practices. I encourage you to create your own rituals and ceremonies to help you design and structure a consistent prayer practice.

MY PERSONAL PRAYER PRACTICE IS VARIED, drawing on several time tested techniques. Being mindful, repeating an interior mantra, and frequently pausing in stillness to observe what is actively present around me, are my day to day, moment to moment practices. In addition, for three decades I have made a career as a Byzantine-style icon painter of devotional art in the Orthodox tradition. I combine natural powdered pigments from Mother Earth with an egg yolk emulsion called egg tempera. I have learned a great deal about stillness and awe while watching colors settle as paint dries. There is an alchemy in the medium and technique that mirrors reverential respect for the world around me as it unfolds.

Imagine the many moments we miss with our rushing around?
Slow down and ask yourself, where am I trying to go?
What am I trying to achieve?
What do I need to have a full life?

IN MY HOME, I HAVE FASHIONED AN ALTAR. It is actually a small shelf that reshuffles and morphs over time. What I keep there are photos of those I pray for; amulets that symbolize current events; and an ongoing collection of objects and scraps from Mother Earth. It is a mish-mash of thoughts and objects. Walking by throughout the day reminds me to stand still in gratitude, repentance, and compassion; to request guidance for my life on this planet.

How to Use This Book

The book may be used for individual personal prayer or communal prayer. In addition to your own personal prayer practice, it is my hope that you will gather with others to pray, meditate, reflect, and discuss the texts. When working with a group, I suggest you assign individual readers for the meditations. Select one voice for the opening individual prayer, followed by reading the next section in unison as a group of voices and conclude with one other individual reader as the voice for the Earth Speaks. Alternatng the voices will create a powerful way to listen, reflect, and sustain the attention of everyone involved.

THE BOOK IS DIVIDED INTO FOUR SECTIONS focused on: Gratitude, Repentance, Compassion, and Guidance. The sections can be read individually or several at a time. There is no prescribed order. Each section begins with a scripture reference or quote for meditation, followed by an individual prayer, then a collective prayer, and finally concludes with a response when Earth Speaks.

FORGIVE MY CLUMSY ASSUMPTION that anyone could imagine the Earth's wisdom and grandeur having a single voice humanity can understand. After these meditations I assure you, Creation will appear differently to you.

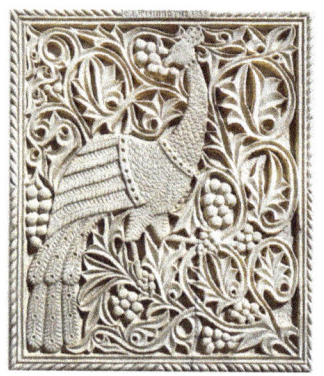

How To Live In A World That Is Dying? by Mary Jane Miller

GRATITUDE

GOING DEEPER WITH GOD IN GRATITUDE will hopefully sensitize your heart to the current condition and vulnerability of our planet. "When we sit quietly in the presence of something greater than ourselves, something happens. Desires pour forth, fears subside, and a supernatural calm floods our being. We are being cared for.

Earth is the rock upon which we live and move and have our being, she is a living organism intimately linked to every part of our experience. She breathes, creates and flourishes as we do. Prayer and supplication with thanksgiving have been the foundation of spiritual life throughout the ages.

IN ANCIENT SCRIPTURE, THE BOOK OF GENESIS OPENS with God giving the whole Earth into our care. God gave Creation to humanity as a gift to have and to hold, similar to a marriage. It is God's magnificent, mysterious love that calls life into being, binds it together, and sustains it. Let us enliven our hearts and minds with gratitude for the Earth and celebrate the gift she is, in both her physical and spiritual existance.

WE HAVE ALL BENEFITED FROM THE ABUNDANCE OF our planetary home. Early saints like St. Hildegard of Bingen, St. Therese of Lisieux, St. Benedict, St. Francis of Assisi, St. Kateri Tekakwitha, St. Aquinas, Teilhard de Chardin, and Origin exalted the wonders of Creation. Their mystical thoughts unanimously concluded what a miracle it is to be alive. It is not redundant or inconsequential for us to pray for, meditate on, and praise all the life forms surrounding us. In fact it is an essential component for living a meaningful life.

THE FOLLOWING REFLECTIONS BEGIN WITH SHORT VERSES to open the heart with prayer, then transition to a collective voice and conclude with Earth's response. To alter one mind at a time is a beginning.

Visible Mystery Is Everywhere

"In the beginning, God created the Heavens and the Earth
and all that is in it. God fashioned Adam from dust
and placed him in the Garden of Eden.
Adam is told that he can eat freely of all the trees in the garden,
except one; the tree of knowledge of good and evil."

Genesis 1

MOTHER EARTH, you brought me into existence as a miracle. Your
planetary home and all life forms have their origin in star dust, when
a supernatural occurrence caused all matter to be. Your limitless potential and
diversity inspires me. Help me to cherish and nurture your earthly
Garden of Eden. Fill me with the grace to know good from evil
and align my soul with the Creator and Creation.

MOTHER EARTH, let us praise and exalt what has been given. Praise you, Divine
Mother, for sustaining your garden that we call home. You have showered the land
with streams of water and warm our lives
with the heat of the sun. Thank you, for the abundant, incredible beauty
that leads us straight to your heart. In gratitude,
we choose to love Creation more each day.

EARTH SPEAKS: Your gratitude is grace, learn that my body is a visible
manifestation of mystery. The natural order is a myriad of secrets knit together and
fused to function as one body. Look at the many species I have created
and be thankful for their great capacity to love and share in my abundance. There is
nothing at your fingertips that I have not given to you.
Respectfully, live in peace with all that exists.

Pray With Praise

"Then God said, 'Let Us make man in Our image, according to
Our likeness; and let them rule over the fish of the sea
and the birds of the sky and the cattle
and over all the Earth,
and over every creeping thing that creeps on the Earth.'"
Genesis 1:26

MOTHER EARTH, you have ordained me from the beginning to realize my place in the cosmos. Yours is the spiritual intelligence that caused me to be. With humility, I acknowledge and celebrate all life on Earth given into my care. In praise and thanksgiving and in your likeness I want to preserve what I did not create. Grant to me a clear and vibrant appreciation for the smallest of insects who hide in the grass, for the greatest whales that migrate in the oceans, and for the herds of wild animals on the African savanna.

MOTHER EARTH, your grace blesses our lives in perpetuity, trusting that Earth has and will constantly renew herself, throughout the millennium. Your divine image and likeness is most evident in the eternal love we share and proclaim. Thank you, for trusting our stewardship to rule over your world with wisdom instead of superiority. Let us be like you and not hinder or limit what you have given into our guardianship.

EARTH SPEAKS: Your gratitude is grace, learn that my body is a visible manifestation of mystery. The natural order is a myriad of secrets knit together and fused to function as one body. Look at the many species I have created and be thankful for their great capacity to love and share in my abundance. There is nothing at your fingertips that I have not given to you. Respectfully, live in peace with all that exists.

It Begins With Something as Small as a Mustard Seed

"What shall we say the kingdom of God is like,
or what parable shall we use to describe it?
It is like a mustard seed, which is the smallest of all seeds on Earth.
Yet when planted, it grows and becomes the largest of all garden plants,
with such big branches that the birds can perch in its shade."
Mark 4:30–32

MOTHER EARTH, what a marvel it is to imagine seeds as kernels that are capable
of receiving all that life offers. They crack open and root at the appointed time and
place to grow in fullness. Creation is full of these microcosms of mystery happening
in every corner of the globe, from one generation to another. In wonder and awe,
I witness the cosmic unfolding of your ways through evolution and rejoice in your
supereminence. Help me to plant seeds of gratitude that honor and cherish
a deepening desire for peace on Earth and good will towards humankind.

MOTHER EARTH, we recognize your wisdom in every seed on every farm and in
every forest, from east to west and north to south. They are examples
of how life begins and then flourishes. Thank you, for the divine spark of life
imbued in them. You have designed them perfectly to survive without
help or alteration from us. And just like them, you have created us
with a treasury of unrealized potential for good.
For this, we give you praise.

EARTH SPEAKS: Your gratitude is grace, learn that my body is a visible
manifestation of mystery. The natural order is a myriad of secrets knit together and
fused to function as one body. Look at the many species I have created
and be thankful for their great capacity to love and share in my abundance.
There is nothing at your fingertips that I have not given to you.
Respectfully, live in peace with all that exists.

The Lilies of the Field Wait
In Stillness and Beauty

"Consider the lilies of the field,
how they grow: they neither toil nor spin,
yet I tell you, even Solomon in all his glory
was not arrayed like one of these."
Matthew 6:28

MOTHER EARTH, thank you for the courage to look toward Heaven, eternity, and not be anxious for tomorrow. You have touched my soul with awareness, as a lily is touched by the light of the sun. Lillies like all flowers open to remind me of purity, unfolding beauty, and rebirth. I see them give themselves to the light without waning. Open my eyes to see your world in stillness and know all this is enough for me at this moment.

MOTHER EARTH, we praise your inextricable commitment to life that blooms and abounds everywhere. Help us to transcend our past and array our souls with bountiful blossoms of gratitude for your body's glory. We acknowledge with grateful hearts the privilege to serve, revere, and watch the splendor of your terrestrial garden evolving as you nurture and preserve it. Teach us to be more appreciative of your Creation and know we are loved.

EARTH SPEAKS: Your gratitude is grace, learn that my body is a visible manifestation of mystery. The natural order is a myriad of secrets knit together and fused to function as one body. Look at the many species I have created and be thankful
for their great capacity to love and share in my abundance.
There is nothing at your fingertips that I have not given to you.
Respectfully, live in peace with all that exists.

Humanity Can Testify

"He did not leave Himself without witness.
He did good and gave you rains from Heaven and fruitful seasons,
satisfying your hearts with food and gladness."
Acts 14:17

MOTHER EARTH, thank you for your fertile lands that are always here
for my good, reminding me daily to live in balance, love, and apprication.
I give you thanks for the beauty of the sea, Earth, and sky. I acknowledge
and praise you for your brilliant equanimity; the rain that falls on the whole Earth
and the sun that gives light and life to all of Creation. My heart exalts your presence
when I hear the sound of birds bathing, gurgling streams,
and the wind that blows pollen from one fruit tree to another.

MOTHER EARTH, grant that we may share in community the grateful
enjoyment of your bountiful eco-systems. We are blessed and fed by you beyond
measure. May our adoration for your Creation rain down humility in our hearts.
We are children of the light by grace, able to live lives of love, joy, peace,
patience, kindness, goodness, faithfulness, gentleness, and self-control.
We are indebted to you and will testify to one another from generation to
generation, in all seasons, and till the end of time.

EARTH SPEAKS: Your gratitude is grace, learn that my body is a visible
manifestation of mystery. The natural order is a myriad of secrets knit together and
fused to function as one body. Look at the many species I have created
and be thankful for their great capacity to love and share in my abundance.
There is nothing at your fingertips that I have not given to you.
Respectfully, live in peace with all that exists.

My Ways Are Not Your Ways

"For my thoughts are not your thoughts, neither are your ways
my ways, declares the LORD.
As the Heavens are higher than the Earth,
so are my ways."
Isaiah 55:8–9

MOTHER EARTH, your endless evolution continues to reveal your secrets for my
understanding. Thank you for your splendid energy that has
rejuvenated and replenished itself through perfect balance and harmony over
millions of centuries. Your grace fills me with a holy obligation to
love the Earth even when I do not know how. Thank you, for my awareness of your
natural order in Creation. Soften my stubborn mind and bestow
on me ever more wisdom to share with those around me.

MOTHER EARTH, may your beauty be a constant presence in every person,
and in every corner of Creation. We are grateful for your generosity
and abundance at the end of the day and live with expectation
till the end of time. Powerful Earth, Creation arose as a majestic event.
Your ways enliven our thoughts to love deeply, move with veneration,
and dance about the planet knowing our time is brief.
We will rejoice in your natural splendor and magnificent domain.

EARTH SPEAKS: Your gratitude is grace, learn that my body is a visible
manifestation of mystery. The natural order is a myriad of secrets knit together and
fused to function as one body. Look at the many species I have created
and be thankful for their great capacity to love and share in my abundance. There is
nothing at your fingertips that I have not given to you.
Respectfully, live in peace with all that exists.

Repentance

JOHN THE BAPTIST WAS RIGHT IN SAYING "repent and prepare ye the way." Repent means to change direction. The time has come for us to reproach ourselves with sorrow for the devastation we have caused. Creation is pleading for our marriage with her to survive. We are her genesis and, like her, are capable of limitless love and self sacrifice, yet we have failed to love and care for her as we are called to do.

LET US ADMIT AND HUMBLY ACKNOWLEDGE our pitiful behavior and repent for what we have done to her natural order. Riches and power cannot fulfill the longing we have to be part of and united with the Divine. Our uncharitable behavior towards each other has hurt and diminished the planet and our species as a whole. What good can come of controlling others and justifying ourselves?

WE ARE GUESTS ON THE PLANET. Getting what we want, when we want, and how we want, creates a great divide between the self and the rest of existence. Our way into the future will digress even more without individual self-reflection and collective repentance. We must consider how we have ignored and forsaken the Earth as our Mother and friend.

THE RAVAGES OF WAR, THE BLOOD STAINED SOIL, and our current love affair with producing weapons of mass destruction is only one theme humanity must address. Can we live with our differences without destruction and annihilation? Human trafficking, the sex trade, displaced migrants, and the abuse of animals are other tragic issues of human denial for contemplation. It is time to slow down and profoundly reflect on our human history and behavior. We cannot go forward without a clear understanding of where we are and how we arrived here.

THE FOLLOWING REFLECTIONS begin with short verses to open the heart with prayer, then transition to a collective voice and conclude with Earth's response. To alter one mind at a time is a beginning.

We Will Become a New Creation

"On Earth, as it is in Heaven. Do you not know?
Have you not heard?
The everlasting God, the Lord, and Creator of the Earth
did not become weary or tired.
His understanding is inscrutable."
Isaiah 40:28

GREAT MOTHER of Diversity, heaven and Earth are weary of my ignorance. Teach me a new way to live on Earth without causing devastation or hostility so the beauty that has been lost is restored. Through my shame, I will awaken without lassitude to my habitual, mindless consumption thatcauses excessive waste.
With a contrite heart, I am sorry for not protecting clean air, preserving the rainforests, and safeguarding crystal-clear water.
Holy Spirit, come, show me the courage to foster new ways to safeguard the planet.

GREAT MOTHER of Diversity, we are filled with remorse for our behavior.
We have been a hindrance to sustainable life around the globe.
Contrition drives us to beseech the heavens for ideas to replenish what we have regrettably depleted. Forgive us for not holding our leaders and industrial giants accountable for their waste and negligent behavior.
We have turned a blind eye to the greed that benefits a few at the deprivation of many, including Creation.

EARTH SPEAKS: Make a new covenant with me. Repent and redirect your mind.
The love and life I give freely to you and all of Creation is inexhaustible.
Cherish it for those who will come after you. I see your actions and disgraceful reckless behavior that has no regard for future generations.
Your children will live with the choices you make today.
Take heed, this world is not yours–it is borrowed.
You have abused and depleted me, yet, I am eternal and will replenish myself. I will forgive your ignorance and teach you the depths of my mercy.

I Will Restore Their Lands

"Then if my people humble themselves,
pray, and turn from their wicked ways,
I will hear from Heaven and
will forgive their sins and restore their land."
2 Chronicles 7:14

GREAT MOTHER of Diversity, forgive me for my lies, waste, ignorance,
and sloth. Mother Earth, heal and emancipate my thoughtless behaviors.
I repent for impeding the natural laws that govern your lands.
My soul is filled with regret for asking for more than I need and
selfishly withholding the abundance you have shared with me.
I have forgotten your witness is always with me, deep in my heart and mind.
No outside force can change me, I know my heart needs to be restored.

GREAT MOTHER of Diversity, we regret our disregard for the
destruction we cause and ask for the courage to change our ways. We have taken
freely of God's created order and sadly diminished
the privilege of life for the smallest of creatures. Our landfills are full,
the oceans die beneath the endless transport of goods from shore to shore,
and our fields are scorched with pesticides.
Help us to see the error of our ways, the harm we have done, and
the destruction we have left in our wake upon Creation. Recognizing
our cruelty will be the foundation for our repentance and sorrow.

EARTH SPEAKS: Make a new covenant with me. Repent and redirect your mind.
The love and life I give freely to you and all of Creation
is inexhaustible. Cherish it for those who will come after you.
I see your actions and disgraceful reckless behavior that has no regard for future
generations. Your children will live with the choices you make today.
Take heed, this world is not yours–it is borrowed.
You have abused and depleted me, yet, I am eternal and
will replenish myself. I will forgive your ignorance and teach you
the depths of my mercy.

Love Without Fear

"I need not fear terror that stalks in the night,
the arrow that flies in the day,
plague that strikes in the darkness,
or calamity that destroys at noon."
Psalm 91:5-6

GREAT MOTHER of Diversity, bless me with the courage to see beyond
the consequences of fear, plague, calamity, and tribulations I live with.
I am ignorant of God's blueprint, design, arrangement, and pattern for how all this
came into being. Remorse gives me a robust awareness to ponder how I have lived
outside of relationship with and responsibility for your planet.
My shame brings darkness, death, and isolation when I blame others
and refuse to learn from my own transgressions.

GREAT MOTHER of Diversity, we choose your light and truth instead of fear. For
too long, we have dominated and controlled and brought darkness and fear upon the
creatures that live on sea and shore. Instead of using our minds
to regenerate the soil, enhance the harvest, and become ambassadors
of perpetual life, we have lived for money, power, and dominance.
Our interior lives have not earned us the grace and beauty
Creation possesses. Our fears have corroded and brought abuse
upon the land, sea, and air. We are sorry.

EARTH SPEAKS: Make a new covenant with me. Repent and redirect your mind.
The love and life I give freely to you and all of Creation
is inexhaustible. Cherish it for those who will come after you. I see
your actions and disgraceful reckless behavior that has no regard for future
generations. Your children will live with the choices you make today.
Take heed, this world is not yours–it is borrowed.
You have abused and depleted me, yet, I am eternal and
will replenish myself. I will forgive your ignorance and teach you
the depths of my mercy.

Peace From Above

"A new day will dawn on us from above…
He will give light to those who live in the dark
and in death's shadow.
He will guide us into the path of peace."
Luke 1:78-80

GREAT MOTHER of Diversity, you don't condemn me
and you won't disown me; I am your child forever.
Yet, I look upon Creation with sorrow.
I have crippled and poisoned natural resources by tailoring them
to my benefit. Forgive me for disrupting the natural order which has been
established through the light of your wisdom and peace.
I will stop my willfulness that hurts and undermines the health and
wellbeing of this planet. I take full responsiblitiy for my misbehavior.

GREAT MOTHER of Diversity, fill us with sorrowful recognition to adopt
new perspectives that unite our efforts with the divine energy
that set this all in motion. Our independence and isolation from you
and one another is shameful. Mother Earth, you witness our trauma,
abuse, and condemnations that cause our night fears and terror
about the future. The shadow of death compels us to join hands,
breathe, and move together in search of your light and wisdom.

EARTH SPEAKS: Make a new covenant with me. Repent and redirect your mind.
The love and life I give freely to you and all of Creation
is inexhaustible. Cherish it for those who will come after you. I see
your actions and disgraceful reckless behavior that has no regard for future
generations. Your children will live with the choices you make today.
Take heed, this world is not yours–it is borrowed.
You have abused and depleted me, yet, I am eternal and
will replenish myself. I will forgive your ignorance and teach you
the depths of my mercy.

Nothing Lasts Forever

"Know well the condition of your flocks and
pay attention to your herds; for wealth does not
last forever, nor does a crown endure for all generations.
When the grass disappears, the new growth is seen,
and the herbs of the mountains are gathered in,
the lambs will be for your clothing, and the goats will bring
the price of a field, and there will be goats' milk
enough for your food."
Proverbs 27:23-26

GREAT MOTHER of Diversity, I have held too tightly to the idea
that nothing changes. You unceasingly give me everything I need to thrive in this
world, yet my fears of losing what I create is debilitating. My life does not consist of
permanent situations that I can possess or control any more
than your Creation exists at a standstill.
Nothing lasts forever, loss is part of life, and change is letting go.
Your creative spirit is everlasting, and my participation
is but a brush stroke in an ever changing landscape.

GREAT MOTHER of Diversity, your kind-heartedness holds the power
over life and death. We have failed to trust catastrophes
that enable new beginnings. Forgive our ignorance and efforts
to subjugate the eco-systems, ravage and control resources, and devastate
the biological balance. We are making it harder every year
for anything to flourish. The cosmos was not created as a place to waste
but formed with the potential for rejuvenation, evolution,
and the marvel of unexpected transformation.

Earth Speaks: Make a new covenant with me. Repent and redirect your mind. The
love and life I give freely to you and all of Creation
is inexhaustible. Cherish it for those who will come after you.
I see your actions and disgraceful reckless behavior that has no regard for future
generations. Your children will live with the choices you make today.
Take heed, this world is not yours–it is borrowed.
You have abused and depleted me, yet, I am eternal and
will replenish myself. I will forgive your ignorance and teach you
the depths of my mercy.

Generously Give to God

"Give to the Most High as he has given,
and give with generosity from what you have, because
the Lord is the one who repays, and he will repay you
seven times over. Don't offer a bribe, because the Lord won't
accept it. Don't present an unrighteous sacrifice,
because the Lord will judge, and show no partiality.
God will listen to the complaint of those who are wronged.
God will never ignore an orphan's plea,
nor that of a widow when she pours out a complaint."
Sirach 35:12-17

GREAT MOTHER of Diversity, I know the injustice I have contributed
to Creation, therefore, let me not grumble when the polar caps melt,
the fires rage, and new growth is thwarted. My heart has failed
to discern the difference between what is sacred and the moments,
places, and things I desecrate in your sight. At times I violate and defile your
environment through my lack of reverence. Lead me with prudence
to nurture a new self, one that knows righteousness without fear
and celebrates the holiness which sustains truth.

GREAT MOTHER of Diversity, give us hearts of repentance for the
wrongs we have done to you. The time has come for us to stop and know
ourselves again as a new creation. When the well is dry and the water
polluted, when the mountains of garbage, waste, and greed clog
all the systems, direct our hearts to admit past paradigms
no longer work. Let us fearlessly aspire to infuse new patterns
of sustainability around the globe and trust that all will be well.

EARTH SPEAKS: Make a new covenant with me. Repent and redirect your mind. The
love and life I give freely to you and all of Creation
is inexhaustible. Cherish it for those who will come after you. I see
your actions and disgraceful reckless behavior that has no regard for future
generations. Your children will live with the choices you make today.
Take heed, this world is not yours–it is borrowed.
You have abused and depleted me, yet, I am eternal and
will replenish myself. I will forgive your ignorance and teach you
the depths of my mercy.

Compassion

CREATION IS NOT A ONE-TIME EVENT but instead a process of evolution. The animals, insects, forests, fish in the sea, and beings that fly are all living symphonies interconnected and harmonious. Just as music communicates its beauty through many connected notes to create a symphony, we and all of Creation are a symphony of connections.

OUR SOCIETIES HAVE LOST COMPASSIONATE CONNECTIONS to each other and the Earth. This era is calling humanity to acknowledge our participation in the splintered relationships we ignore around the globe. The divisions between us are widening. We cannot continue to live lives of inequality, conflict, and war when the stakes are so high.

SAINT FRANCIS HAD THE UNCOMMON PRACTICE of referring to animals, plants, and elements as "brother" and "sister." This was because he could see himself as part of the whole. His mystical understanding called all aspects of Creation the children of God, impregnated with dignity and honor. He referred to the mountain, forests, and seas as family members.

OUR HUMANE CAPACITY TO NURTURE EACH OTHER AND CREATION is unsurpassed. Blame will only serve to divide us further. Merging our differences with compassion and humble acknowledgment of our behavior will change us. Sharing our sadness and admitting what has been lost is the beginning of truth. Together as a species, we can guide one another and bring healing to the Earth.

COMPASSION IS MORE THAN AWARENESS–IT IS FORGIVENESS. Change begins with one thought and one person at a time. Always imagine yourself walking in another's shoes with meekness, forgiving injustices, and forgiving ourselves. Our hearts and minds must grow in the direction of desired peace, wholeness, generosity, love, and gratitude if we are to turn our global crisis around.

The following reflections begin with short verses to open the heart with prayer, then transition to a collective voice and conclude with Earth's response.
To alter one mind at a time is a beginning.

Same Divine Energy

"A generous heart, kind speech, and a life of service
are the things which renew humanity."
Gautama Buddha

UNWAVERING SPIRIT, bless me with mercy to see the benevolent
patterns that course through Creation and that are reflected in our
human commonality. Let my small acts of kindness and sympathy unite with
millions of people to transform the world. Grant me the
capacity to be sympathetic with what others are feeling. Help me to reshape my heart
with understanding for them. Inspire me to serve where I am called and nurture new
connections and possibilities yet unseen.

UNWAVERING SPIRIT, every race, creed, and color of human being was created
by and through the same divine energy. We will be gathered in the end
to the same benevolent maker. We are helplessly entwined in a spiritual revelation
that is materializing. We ourselves have suffered the consequences left to us
by previous generations, and still we willfully ignore the legacy we leave
for those that will follow. Awaken our mercy and fill us
with compassion for the generations to come.

Earth Speaks: I have orchestrated the way for all living things to be
interconnected. They thrive on and are dependent on not being a hindrance
to any other living thing. Take all of me with prudence
and respect for I am your source of life. Can you see the magnitude of
love I have for what I have created? You, too, will love me as you
come to love yourself and one another. You and I are gifts for one another,
to share and cultivate our potential with compassion.

Make a New Covenant With Earth

"We exchanged the truth about God for a lie.
We worshiped and served our created things
rather than the Creator."
Romans 1:25

UNWAVERING SPIRIT, help me merge my personal values with your
perfect order to bring about an alchemy that heals my ignorance. Help me to grow in
awareness of the animal kingdom and its glory.
Any affliction they endur is also mine.
Comfort and heal my isolation from their demise and give me corage to see the truth
of their struggle. Let me venerate Earth with a new covenant
rejoicing in all your flora and fauna
to love with mercy what I did not create.

UNWAVERING SPIRIT, instill in us a desire to belong to one another, to be rooted
in service, and to live ethical lives sharing your terrestrial home. What is good for
humanity is not necessarily good for the planet.
Give us compassionate wisdom and respect for the creatures who give their lives
for us. Cows, pigs, and chickens live in deplorable conditions waiting to die for our
benefit, and we call it nourishment.
Fish, shrimp, and salmon are packed tightly into the smallest of areas
to grow, having never seen the vastness of the oceans, rivers, or seas.
Guide us in cultivating food sources that keep a balance between
flora and fauna; to cherish the privilege of their living
with us on your planetary home.

EARTH SPEAKS: I have orchestrated the way for all living things to be
interconnected. They thrive on and are dependent on not being a hindrance
to any other living thing. Take all of me with prudence
and respect for I am your source of life. Can you see the magnitude of
love I have for what I have created? You, too, will love me as you
come to love yourself and one another. You and I are gifts for one another,
to share and cultivate our potential with compassion.

We Have Been Called by Name

"Lift your eyes on high and see. The One who leads calls the stars by name; because of the greatness of His might and the strength of His power. Not one of them is missing."

Isaiah 40:26

UNWAVERING SPIRIT, you have given me eyes to see, ears to listen,
an extraordinary mind, and a heart that beats with love and desire.
With regret, I forget to notice the ways you love, parent, and succor every
aspect of Creation. Teach me to appreciate that nothing
has come into being that has not been called into being. Let me greet all beings
and all living things with humility and holy respect.

UNWAVERING SPIRIT, you care for the air and water, land and sea, from
the mountains to shorelines, and from the rain forests to the river delta.
Our disregard for their fragile ecosystems has caused filth on your
shore lines, oil spills in your oceans, and regretfully, the extinction of
your species around the globe. Our sadness and admission for what
has been lost is our reckoning. Your unseen intelligent spirit preserves them all.
Open our hearts to cherish and treat them with sensitivity.

EARTH SPEAKS: I have orchestrated the way for all living things to be
interconnected. They thrive on and are dependent on not being a hindrance
to any other living thing. Take all of me with prudence
and respect for I am your source of life. Can you see the magnitude of
love I have for what I have created? You, too, will love me as you
come to love yourself and one another. You and I are gifts for one another,
to share and cultivate our potential with compassion.

We Have Been Created
From the Invisible

"By faith, we understand that the worlds were prepared by the word of God, so that what we see was not made out of things visible but rather things invisible."
Hebrews 11:3

UNWAVERING SPIRIT, help me to trust the invisible, unknown,
unpredictable, and unperceived. How can I possibly know the mind of the Maker
and what is right in His unseen world?
Steep mountain slopes, sand dunes, and canyon walls are
held together with an invisible energy of balance and harmony.
Ants, flies, maggots, beetles, mites, and butterflies all flourish
in communion because of your unseen intelligence.
Help me to see there is an energetic spirit coursing through
every molecule in the universe.

UNWAVERING SPIRIT, we have used and abused your animal kingdom
to create abundance for ourselves. Guide us to realize that like us
animals are conscious beings and are precious to you. We need not cause them to
suffer for our benefit. Help us to see that
when we diminish their dignity, we also diminish our own
and yours. Council us to reflect deeply on the noble principles
that preserve the flora and fauna, us, and
Creation alive without blemish.

EARTH SPEAKS: I have orchestrated the way for all living things to be
interconnected. They thrive on and are dependent on not being a hindrance
to any other living thing. Take all of me with prudence
and respect for I am your source of life. Can you see the magnitude of
love I have for what I have created? You, too, will love me as you
come to love yourself and one another. You and I are gifts for one another,
to share and cultivate our potential with compassion.

You Are a Temple

"Don't you realize that your body is the temple of the Holy Spirit,
who lives in you and was given to you by God?
You do not belong to yourself."
1 Corinthians 6:19

Compassion

UNWAVERING SPIRIT, my body is a sacred space where the miracle
of consciousness abides. Guide me in remembering my body
is a temple of spiritual energy and is hyper-connected to life on Earth.
Your benevolent grace is on loan for my well-being. Help me to discern
with empathy the natural habitats, and global resources
so prevelant in your domain.

UNWAVERING SPIRIT, our human power and majesty has dominated
the landscape without compassion around the globe.
We have allowed our differences to divide our house and family.
Help us to see that diversity between cultures, ethnicities, and religious
practice reflects the vast splendor of your Creation. Yours is pure tolerance
and tender care without judgment. Sadly, between our families,
friends, and neighbors we have been insensitive and unkind.
We have forgotten every life is home to a soul.

EARTH SPEAKS: I have orchestrated the way for all living things to be
interconnected. They thrive on and are dependent on not being a hindrance
to any other living thing. Take all of me with prudence
and respect for I am your source of life. Can you see the magnitude of
love I have for what I have created? You, too, will love me as you
come to love yourself and one another. You and I are gifts for one another,
to share and cultivate our potential with compassion.

We Belong Here

"You alone are the Lord. You have inspired the Heavens, the Earth,
the seas, and all that is in them. You give life to all and
the heavenly host is silent before You."
Nehemiah 9:6

UNWAVERING SPIRIT, my soul was placed in the womb of my mother, I was connected to her as I am connected to Creation. Help me surrender my concerns for today and know the life I love and cherish is of your making, generous and without end. Let me be silenced to consider the glory of your planet, to contemplate with empathy your health and wellbeing. With humility I can admit your Creation could exist without me and all of humanity.

UNWAVERING SPIRIT, Creation is not an accident, it is a divinely inspired gift. Let silent awe be our response. Earth and sky support life in abundance. Your oceans and subterranean kingdoms are silent yet are teaming with life. You have deemed humankind as your finest creation and given us more than adequate power to rule. Let us govern with love because love is life's binding force and the highest frequency. Help us to walk gently with compassion upon your Earth.

EARTH SPEAKS: I have orchestrated the way for all living things to be interconnected. They thrive on and are dependent on not being a hindrance to any other living thing. Take all of me with prudence and respect for I am your source of life. Can you see the magnitude of love I have for what I have created? You, too, will love me as you come to love yourself and one another. You and I are gifts for one another, to share and cultivate our potential with compassion.

Guidance

ALBERT EINSTEIN SAID, "We cannot solve problems with the same thinking we used when we created them…" To care lovingly for God's gift is not a monumental job, it simply requires our awareness and a little time from each of us every day. When we ask why we are here and how we are shaping our terrestrial home, our honest conclusions might feel uncomfortable, but, this is the perfect place to begin.

As Pope John Paul II said, "If we scan the regions of our planet, we immediately see that humanity has disappointed God's expectations. Humankind, especially in this era has without hesitation devastated wooded plains and valleys, polluted waters, disfigured the earth's habitat, and made the air unbreathable. We must therefore encourage and support the 'ecologicalconversion' which in recent decades has made humanity more sensitive to the catastrophe to which it has been heading".

It is easy to become overwhelmed with the enormity of the problem. With Divine guidance, we can be better stewards of this extraordinary planet. Meditation and prayer focuses one's desires and begins the "ecological conversion" John Paul II spoke of, one where we listen to the Earth and her lamentations.

Sir David Frederick Attenborough is an example of someone dedicated to giving guidance and inspiration for humanity to live in an era of complexity. He is an English broadcaster, biologist, natural historian, and author. He passionately labors to heighten our awareness through his documentaries about global warming and the loss of vital wildlife habitats. He is an activist and catalyst prompting humanity to wake up to a more appreciative use of Mother Earth.

God knows and Creation knows the magnificent love that binds life together. Creation is a wise teacher. She has in her design what we need for our enlightenment and continued evolution towards being children of the light. All we need to do is take time to reflect, observe, testify, and contemplate her wonders. We have the power to refrain from hindering the natural order that intimately connects us to one another and the world.

The following reflections begin with short verses to open the heart with prayer, then transition to a collective voice and conclude with Earth's response. To alter one mind at a time is a beginning

Spirit of Truth Come

"When the Spirit of truth comes, He will guide you into all truth.
He will not speak on his own but will tell you what He has heard.
He will tell you about the future."
John 16:13

BLESSED ONE Who Nurtures, I humbly beseech you to guide me in becoming an appreciative steward of Earth's riches, a sage of reconciliation between nations and cultures around the globe. Let me beat on heaven's door for the wisdom of truth to honor all life forms with gentleness. Great Spirit of Earth. Counsel my human ignorance and guide me in fashioning a new, consonant relationship with Creation. The Spirit of Truth abides in me and whispers to those who listen.

BLESSED ONE Who Nurtures, how majestic is Earth amid all the other celestial bodies! Council us with ways to live hereafter in harmony with the natural order. Enlighten us with the courage to acknowledge the problems that threaten our survival and the tragic disarray we have created. We will listen with care to the rumblings of Earth, volcanoes, earthquakes, mudslides, and thunder that notify us of what is coming. Guide us in decency and noble thinking to influence a new truth for humanity.

EARTH SPEAKS: Bless you and keep you for I am with you,
I hear your supplications and fears, I will never leave you or crush your desire.
Join me as I pray and intercede with you, for ourselves, and others.
I hold the responsibility for life and ask for your participation,
because my wisdom will become yours one day. We are in this
together till the end of my age and yours. The prayer that turns the world
upside down and sometimes overlooked
is a line in the Lord's prayer,
"thy will be done, on Earth as it is in Heaven"

We Cannot Exhaust
the Love of God

"Ask, and it will be given to you. Seek, and you will find.
Knock, and the door will be opened to you."
Matthew 7:7

Blessed One Who Nurtures, you did not form me to exist in isolation.
Help me to recognize the awe and wonder around me and to escape my lonely
existence. Living in peace with everyone and every living creature is my desire. Guide
me to seek and open doors to solutions and technologies that will develope and
maintain an integrated communion with the natural order.
Advise me on how to participate in advancing emerging
solutions to heal the planet.

Blessed One Who Nurtures, your endless service to the natural order
is filled with love for what you create. Yours is one sacred universe,
and we are part of it. Let us encourage one another to ask and seek love with one
mind and purpose. Help us to merge our love with all life
and as neighbors to share it around your world. We cannot exhaust
the potential for limitless solutions to what is left open to us.
With your help, we shall knock on heaven's door for the wisdom
to use resources rightly with respect for all life on the planet.

Earth Speaks: I am timeless. I will be here long after you have gone.
Humble yourselves when you exhaust resources, devastate the land,
and contaminate the air. You cannot own me, dominate, or reign over
the land and sea. I feel every bit of pain you cause me. Since the
beginning, I have nurtured and replenished myself, even under
the increasing stress and demands humanity places upon me.
Decay and death are my friends, so fear not all will be made well.
Every day you are a new creation with a new mind.
Be prudent with the power you have and do not waste one precious second.

Planting and Reaping

"In the morning sow your seed, and in the evening
do not let your hand be idle. For you do not know which seeds
will be successful, or whether both alike will turn out well."
Ecclesiastes 11:6

BLESSED ONE Who Nurtures, counsel my efforts in being a responsible steward
and participant in the Earth's preservation. Guide me to plant seeds that will
contribute to amiable conservations that safeguard what is vulnerable. Your guidance
assures me that I am a holy servant of the harvest. Mother, comfort and liberate me
from obsessing over my wants, needs, and desires for more or better. Liberate my
selfishness and the constant fear that I will not have enough.

BLESSED ONE Who Nurtures, you made us rulers over the works of your hands
and put everything under our feet–all the flocks and herds
and the animals of the wild, the birds in the sky and all that swim the paths of the
seas. Guide our efforts to preserve, protect, and venerate that which surrounds us,
from the smallest microorganism to the outer reaches of space. Give us strong minds
and hearts to trust your constant generosity, regardless of circumstance.
Help us to administer new ethical
and ecological institutions that are praiseworthy in the ways
we treat your ancient habitat. Inspire in us a knowledgeable trust
that we are absolutely complete now.

EARTH SPEAKS: Bless you and keep you for I am with you,
I hear your supplications and fears, I will never leave you or crush your desire.
Join me as I pray and intercede with you, for ourselves, and others.
I hold the responsibility for life and ask for your participation,
because my wisdom will become yours one day. We are in this
together till the end of my age and yours. The prayer that turns the world
upside down and sometimes overlooked
is a line in the Lord's prayer,
"thy will be done, on Earth as it is in Heaven"

We Are Seen

"The whole of Creation is the place to encounter God.
As our eyes open to the holiness of Creation, we see that
there is nothing trivial or worthless. Rather, all created things
point beyond themselves to their Creator."
Franciscan Sister Ilia Delio

BLESSED ONE Who Nurtures, open my eyes to know the glory of this planet's rejuvenating power and capacity for healing. Guide my heart to comprehend how Creation is looking back at me with guidance and love. I am loved by the natural world–sea and shore, mountain and valley, river and forest–they all see me. They rejoice with my appreciation of their existence. Call me like a child back to a place of wonder. Holy Mother, help me to dream I am fully human and recall my original beauty and perfection embodied in Creation.

BLESSED ONE Who Nurtures, still, so much of your majesty remains hidden and unseen. Help us to notice the miracles happening at every moment from the smallest worm that crosses a hot rock warmed by the sun, to the moon's light that makes dark shadows on the forest floor. We beseech you to orchestrate a new humane reverence for your grand cosmos, set in motion, and always changing. Help us to be still and witness the magnitude of life unfurling within inches of our touch. Council and inspire us to open our eyes and breathe in the glory and wonder of it all.

EARTH SPEAKS: I am timeless. I will be here long after you have gone. Humble yourselves when you exhaust resources, devastate the land, and contaminate the air. You cannot own me, dominate, or reign over the land and sea. I feel every bit of pain you cause me. Since the beginning, I have nurtured and replenished myself, even under the increasing stress and demands humanity places upon me. Decay and death are my friends, so fear not all will be made well. Every day you are a new creation with a new mind. Be prudent with the power you have and do not waste one precious second.

Be Not Afraid

"And do not be afraid of those who kill the body, they cannot kill
the soul. Aren't two sparrows sold for a small coin?
Yet, not one of them falls to the ground without your
Heavenly Father's knowledge. So do not be afraid;
you are worth more than many sparrows."
Matthew 10:28-31

Blessed One Who Nurtures,   you protect me in times of suffering or hardship. Give me strength to challenge injustice, regardless of the situation or persons involved, be they my family, civil servants, or religious leaders. Help me to instruct those around me without anguish when I confront and speak to those in authority. When I ask for direction, you will reveal ways to intervene, protect, or allow what is right. Drive my imaginings with confidence to reshape my life without iniquity or angst of isolation. Your presence is always with me, parenting my true self, those around me, and the world.

Blessed One Who Nurtures,   your love for Creation is new every day at dawn and your tender caress is with us through the night. Guide us to not be overwhelmed by fear, to live sacramental lives, and to reveal the unseen presence of spirit. How can we live with courage in this world in spite of feeling threatened and vulnerable? We suffer anxiety over not knowing if we have value or contribute anything to your Creation. Remind us that we are each seen and nurtured by the same spirit that keeps all things in their place. Everything we need in this world is right here and right now.

Earth Speaks: Bless you and keep you for I am with you, I hear your supplications and fears, I will never leave you or crush your desire. Join me as I pray and intercede with you, for ourselves, and others. I hold the responsibility for life and ask for your participation, because my wisdom will become yours one day. We are in this together till the end of my age and yours. The prayer that turns the world upside down and sometimes overlooked is a line in the Lord's prayer, "thy will be done, on Earth as it is in Heaven"

I Will Always Be With You

"We fix our eyes not on what is seen, but on what is unseen since
what is seen is temporary, but what is unseen is eternal"
2 Corinthians 4:18

"Have I not commanded you to be strong and courageous?
Do not be afraid; do not be discouraged, for God is with you
wherever you go."
Joshua 1:9

BLESSED ONE Who Nurtures, by your grace and intercessory power, take into your hands my confusion and fears. Expose my need for greater wisdom and renew my soul with hope. Hear my plea for Creation. Keep me, guide me, protect me. You are a safe refuge! I am desperate, in pain, and bound by ignorance in need of your instruction. No person can remove the precious care you have for me. In your hands, any situation can be resolved. The divine love and immense mercies that exist in your heart move Creation.

BLESSED ONE Who Nurtures, instill in us the will to act with kindness towards Creation. When flowers quietly open to the sun's rays, make our laughter and joy contagious for others to rejoice. When the air is still and we see one leaf wiggling on a tree branch, let us remember the millions of overlooked movements happening on Earth with happiness. Yours is an unseen spirit that encompasses all that has been ignored and your light shines upon our darkest fears.

EARTH SPEAKS: I am timeless. I will be here long after you have gone. Humble yourselves when you exhaust resources, devastate the land, and contaminate the air. You cannot own me, dominate, or reign over the land and sea. I feel every bit of pain you cause me. Since the beginning, I have nurtured and replenished myself, even under the increasing stress and demands humanity places upon me. Decay and death are my friends, so fear not all will be made well. Every day you are a new creation with a new mind. Be prudent with the power you have and do not waste one precious second.

New Man With a New Mind

"Therefore, if anyone is in Christ, he is a new creature;
the old things passed away; behold, new things have come."
2 Corinthians 5:17

SPIRIT OF Earth,   I belong to you and the cosmos. Straighten my path
to live a noble life without forsaking the Earth. Advise me,
for my egocentric, independant, and selfish thoughts which separated me
from the natural equilibrium that has been set in place.
To be the same quiet witness you so beautifully possess is my aspiration.
Develop in me a new desire to walk
upon the Earth's crust in humble service.

SPIRIT OF Earth,   help us espouse acts of healing, restoration, and
reconciliation in and through Creation. Ever unfolding, your timeless plan
passes beyond our understanding. Help us to be mindful
of any creativity, expertise, genius, or talent we possess and know
they are gifts to be used to serve. Instill in us new ways to heal
what is broken, violated, or injured, so we can better fulfill
the role of stewardship around the globe.

EARTH SPEAKS: Bless you and keep you for I am with you,
I hear your supplications and fears, I will never leave you or crush your desire.
Join me as I pray and intercede with you, for ourselves, and others.
I hold the responsibility for life and ask for your participation,
because my wisdom will become yours one day. We are in this
together till the end of my age and yours. The prayer that turns the world
upside down and sometimes overlooked
is a line in the Lord's prayer,
"thy will be done, on Earth as it is in Heaven"

Closing Thoughts on a New Eden

"God took the man and put him in the Garden of Eden to work it and take care of it. And God commanded the man, 'You are free to eat from any tree in the garden; but you must not eat from the tree of the knowledge of good and evil, for when you eat of it you will surely die." Genesis 1:15-17

Thich Nhat Hanh said that the trees see us, and the mountains and grass watch us as we walk. His words point us towards a new awareness that there is an ongoing exchange between humanity and Creation. Everything is made from the same stardust, molecules, and energy. Let our human cognizance be our connection to our commonality–all life is recycled energy striving to awaken to the harmony and balance within all of Creation.

I believe that awareness and a change of heart will help us find the courage to open ourselves to a deepening care for the planet. It may take some sacrifice on our part. As Christ said, "Where your heart is, there will be your treasure." If we learn to treasure the wonder of humanity, we will love the natural world that surrounds us. If we treasure the natural world, we will love humanity in all its magnificent diversity.

I long to swim in clean, fresh, spring-fed pools with colorful fish. I long to stand under a waterfall and drink its mist. I want to wander through fields of roses, lavender, and fragrant blooming trees. I desire to pick wholesome fruits and nuts from trees untainted by genetic modifications. I long to eat from pure grain fields free of pesticides.

In closing, Powerful Mother, by your grace and intercessory power, take into your hands my confusion and fears. Holy Spirit expose my need for God and renew my soul with hope. Hear my plea for Creation. Keep me, guide me, protect me, oh safe refuge! You know very well how desperate I am, my pain, and how I am bound by ignorance. In your hands, any situation can be resolved. The divine love and immense mercies that exist in your heart move through Creation. Build in me a temple of compassionate care for humanity and our world.

Suggestions for What I Can Do

Plant a tree in gratitude somewhere on the planet.
Eat less meat.
Be thankful for the animals who gave up their lives when served at your table.
Shop less, waste less, fix what is broken.
Take short showers with joy for the water released from the ancient glaciers.
Wear your clothes longer, wash out the spot instead of washing the whole item.
Take a hike or bike using the time to notice how delightful it is to be on this earth.
Enjoy the rain the water that falls to earth freely
Plant a garden and watch it grow.
Read a book instead of taking up a sport that damages the planet.
Eat at home with loved ones and celebrate their presence.
Install a bird bath and watch the birds.
Buy used instead of new, think about all the work that went into creating a toy or spatula.
Build an altar to the earth and display samples of Earth's glory.
Be grateful for the things humanity has made for your benefit.
Compost your food waste and organic debris from the lawn and garden.
Grow less lawn space, plant trees, or ground cover that do not need a lawnmower, extra water, or fertilizer.

Amen, Be at Peace

For the past millennium, our societal paradigms have fashioned and modified our social structures along with our behavior on the planet. Those structures need to be interwoven in cooperation with living eco-systems for our benefit and that of the environment. Humanity is facing an ever increasing challenge to stay awake and engaged with the catastrophic effect we are having on Earth. It is possible that supplications for ourselves and our world will help open our hearts and renew inspirations based on ancient, honorable wisdom. It is not a quick solution, but it is a place to begin..

About the Author

Mary Jane Miller was born in N.Y. in 1954. She and her husband Valentin Gomez have been full time artists for 40 years, moving between the mountains of Appalachia and the sunny deserts of Mexico. Now, they reside full timein Mexico

By chance and grace these two old souls found a life together writing icons. Mary Jane teaches the lost art of Icon writing as a prayer form as well as the work she does daily in the studio. Valentin embellishes the icons by hand tooling soft metal in a technique called repouse.

Together they preserve a life that strives for harmony, balance and purpose in the heart of Mexico in San Miguel Allende. Amid cobblestone streets, saturated colors, and secret gardens, Mary Jane Miller invites the curious tourist or sojourner into her world of iconography today.

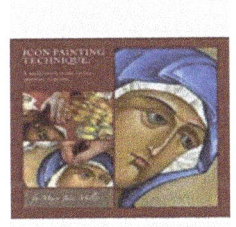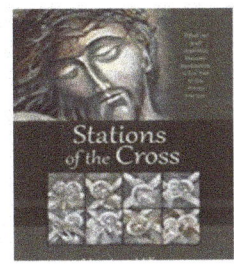

Other Published Works

Life in Christ -The narrative icons and written words are juxtaposed to highlight history, its religious context, and my own inspired reflections. 110-page book that incorporates 30 full-color plates.

Rosary Meditations and Care for Creation -The Joyful Mysteries, Sorrowful Mysteries, Luminous Mysteries, Glorious Mysteries, are all Meditations for humanity. 52 pages of contemporary Rosary Meditations.

In Light of Women -A vibrant text and spectacular icon collection which explores women's images in iconography and their voices in the church. The book describes each images history, religious context and Miller's own reflectionsabout the world we live in today.

Icon Painting Technique -A Journal and Guide to Egg Tempera explains the subtle relationship between the process of icon painting and how it reflects and enriches ones spiritual life.

Books can be purchased on Lulu.com and Amazon.com.

Check out her Websites:
millericons.com, sanmiguelicons.com, sacrediconretreat.com

WE ARE BEING
SEEN

How To Live In A World that is Dying?